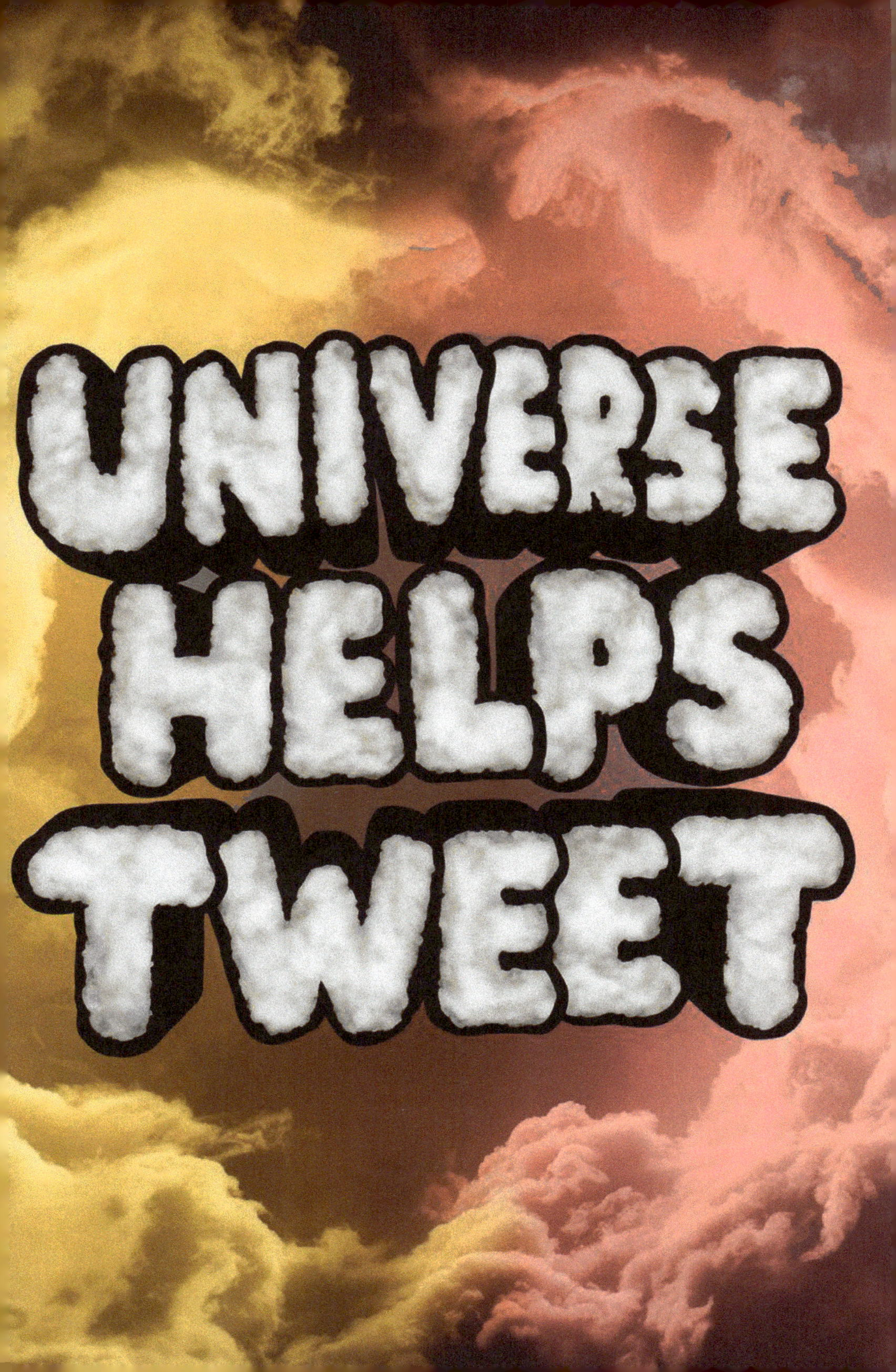
UNIVERSE
HELPS
TWEET

The content associated with this book is the sole work and responsibility of the author. Gatekeeper Press had no involvement in the generation of this content.

Universe Helps Tweet

Published by Gatekeeper Press
7853 Gunn Hwy., Suite 209
Tampa, FL 33626
www.GatekeeperPress.com

ISBN (hardback): 9781662954634

UNIVERSE
HELPS TWEET

LaTarshia McNary

Tampa, Florida

Dedication

"To my mother, who lives amongst the stars.
My mother is my compass, across the Universe and
beyond. May this story reach Her as it travels afar."

"To my children, who continue to inspire me and
keep me believing in my dreams."

"To my family, that helps heal, embrace love,
nurture, and support me."

"To every cosmic being, who saw in me
what I failed to see in myself."

"To the past that emerges me, the present that
elevates me, and the future that evolves me."

"To you, dear reader, for making this journey
an extraordinary adventure."

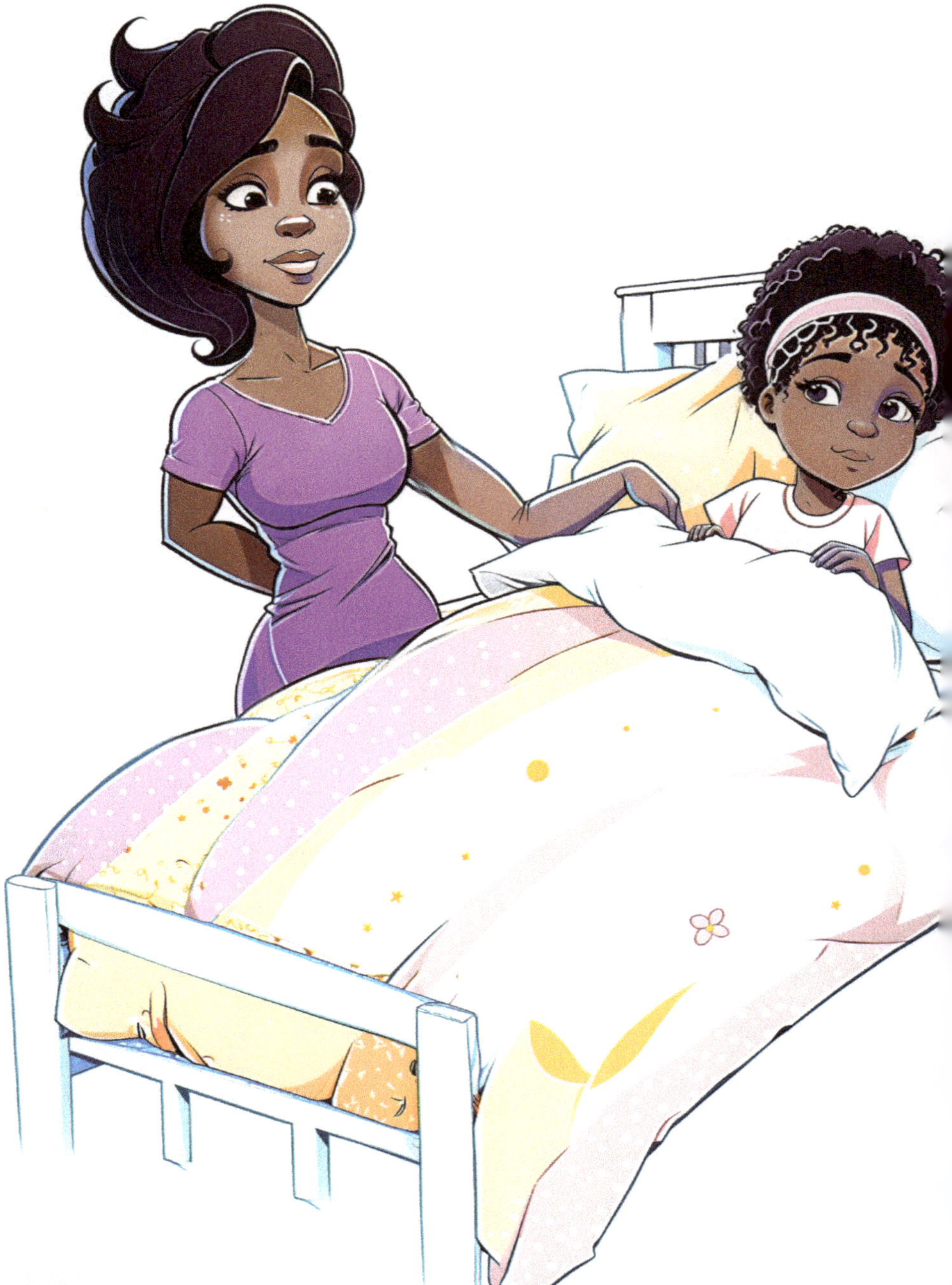

As my mother put me to bed, she said good night. When I closed my eyes, I started to feel **fright**.

DEFINITION

Fright—a sudden feeling of fear

"Mommy, Mommy," Tweet cried out. "I can't sleep. My mind is racing with things that **clutter** my dreams."

DEFINITION
Clutter—a collection of things

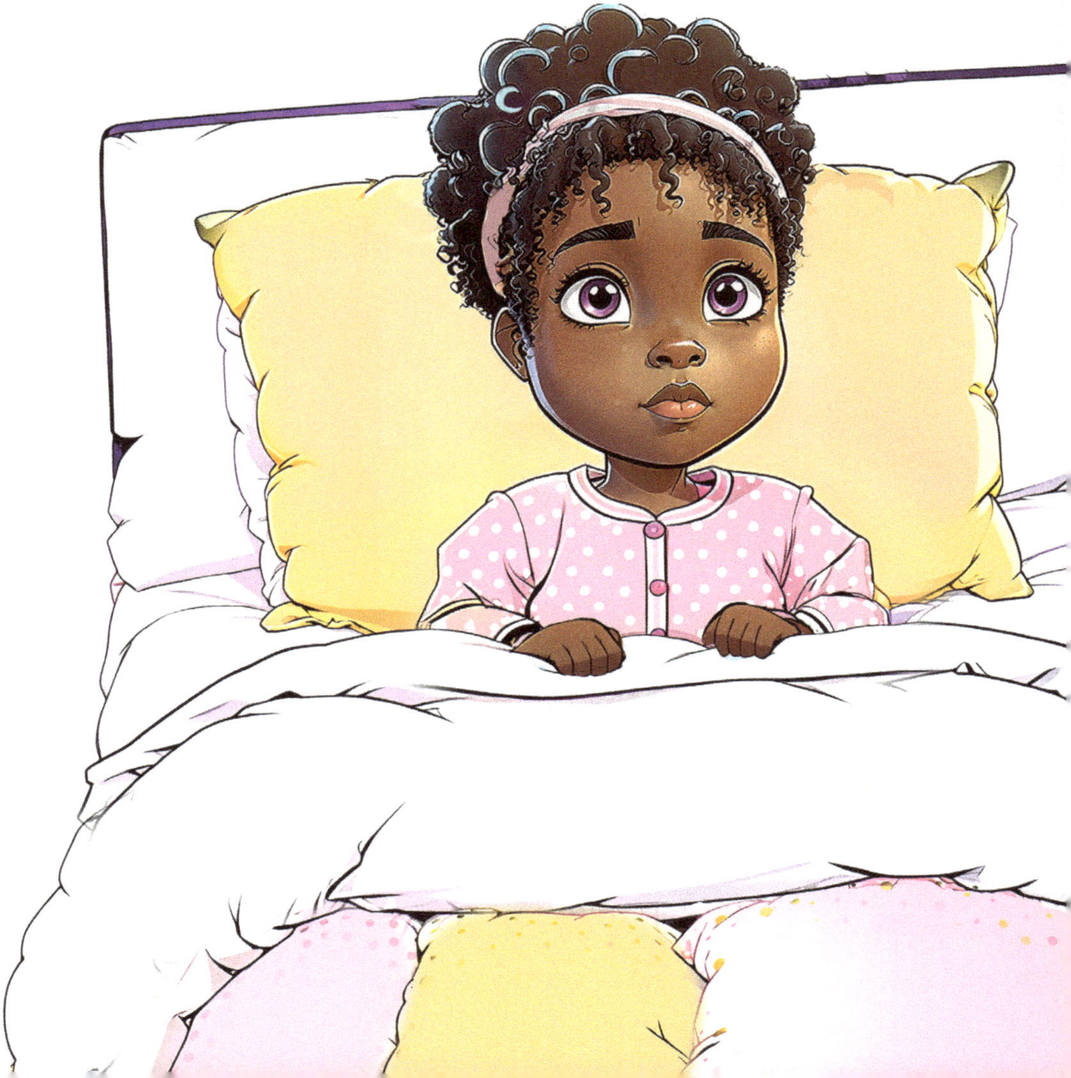

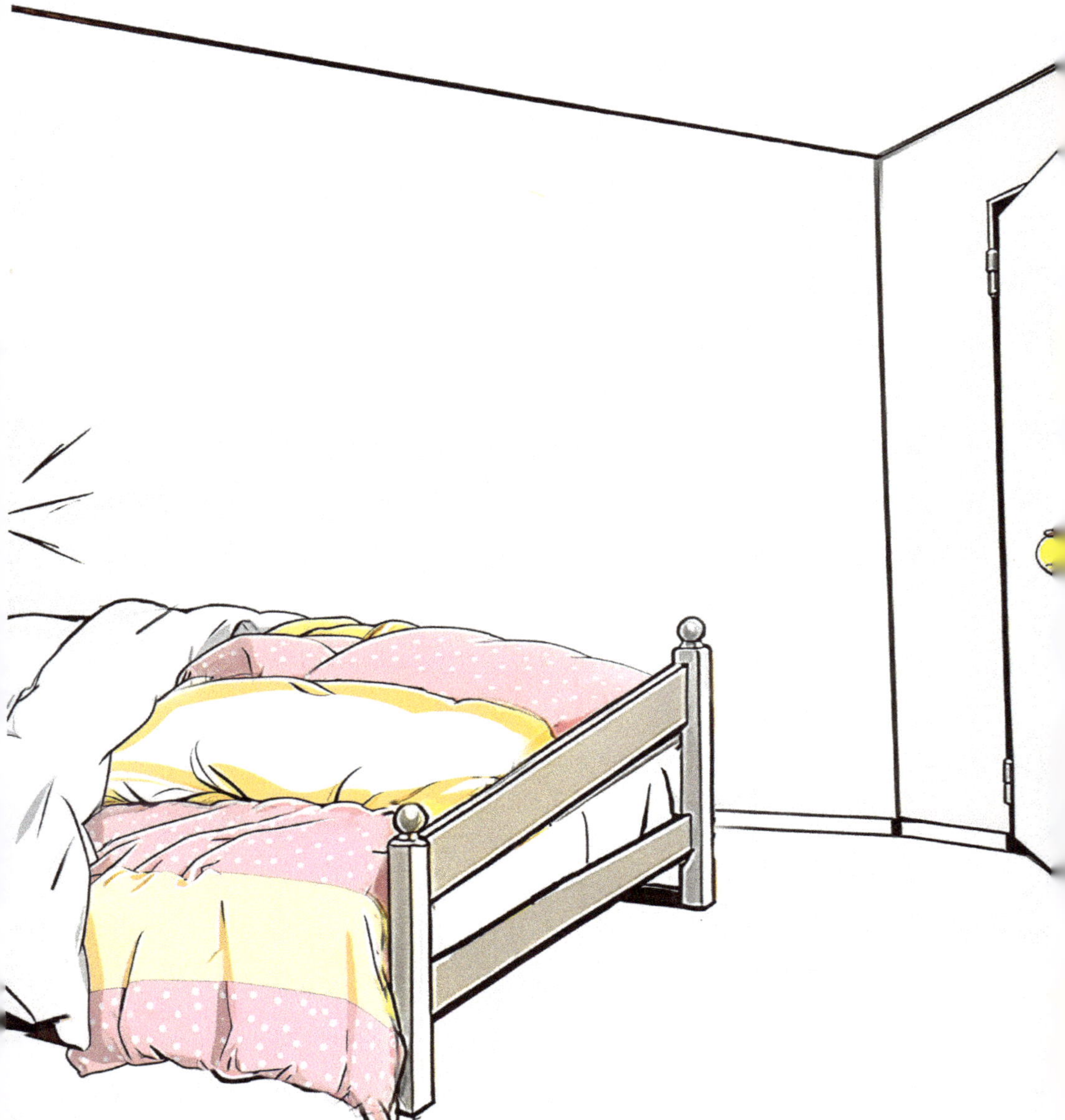

Mother said, "Try closing your eyes and **imagining** sheep, and count them quietly until you're fast asleep."

DEFINITION

Imagining—to form a mental image

As Tweet closed her eyes and
started to imagine sheep,
she counted them quietly until
she fell asleep.

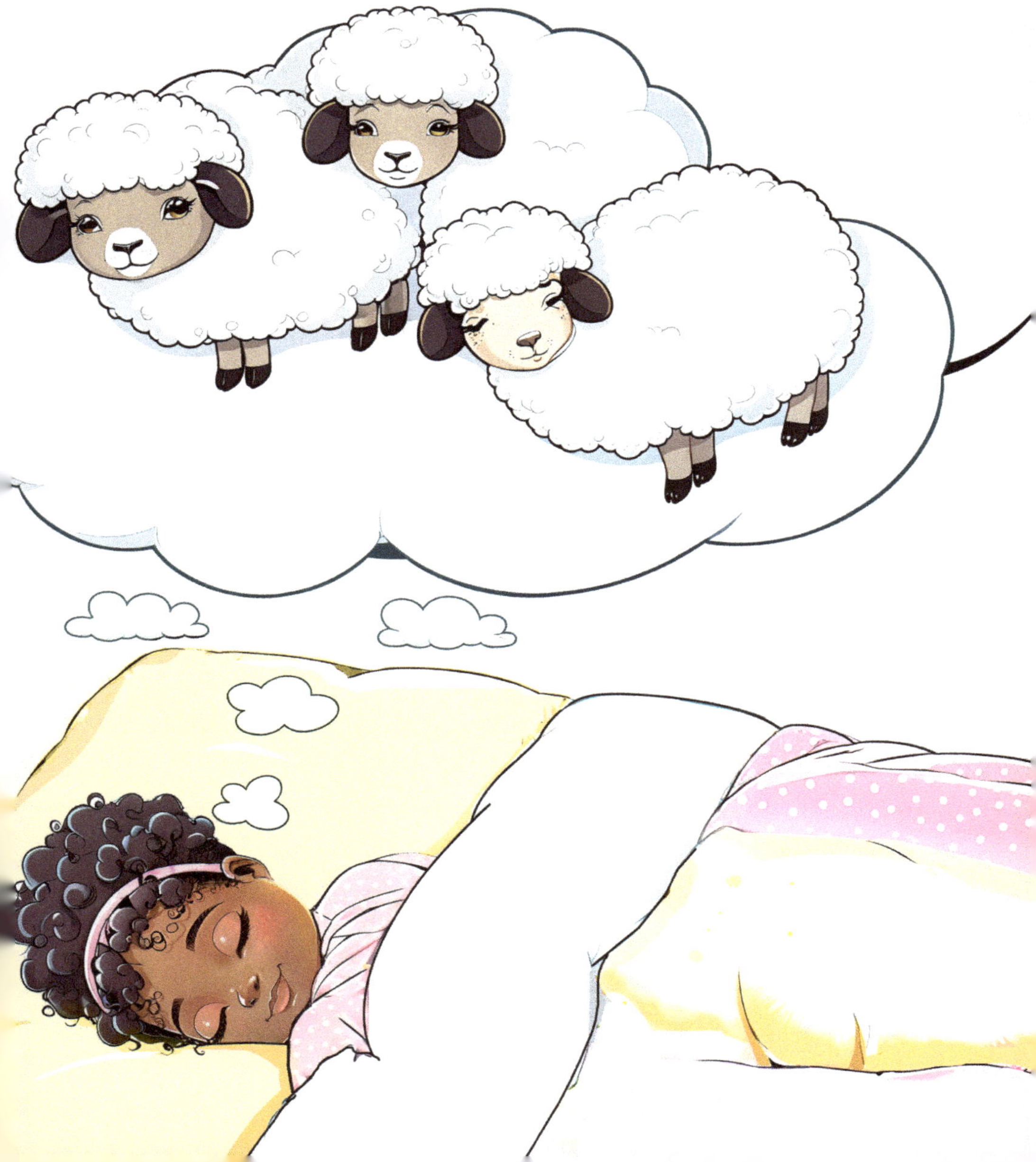

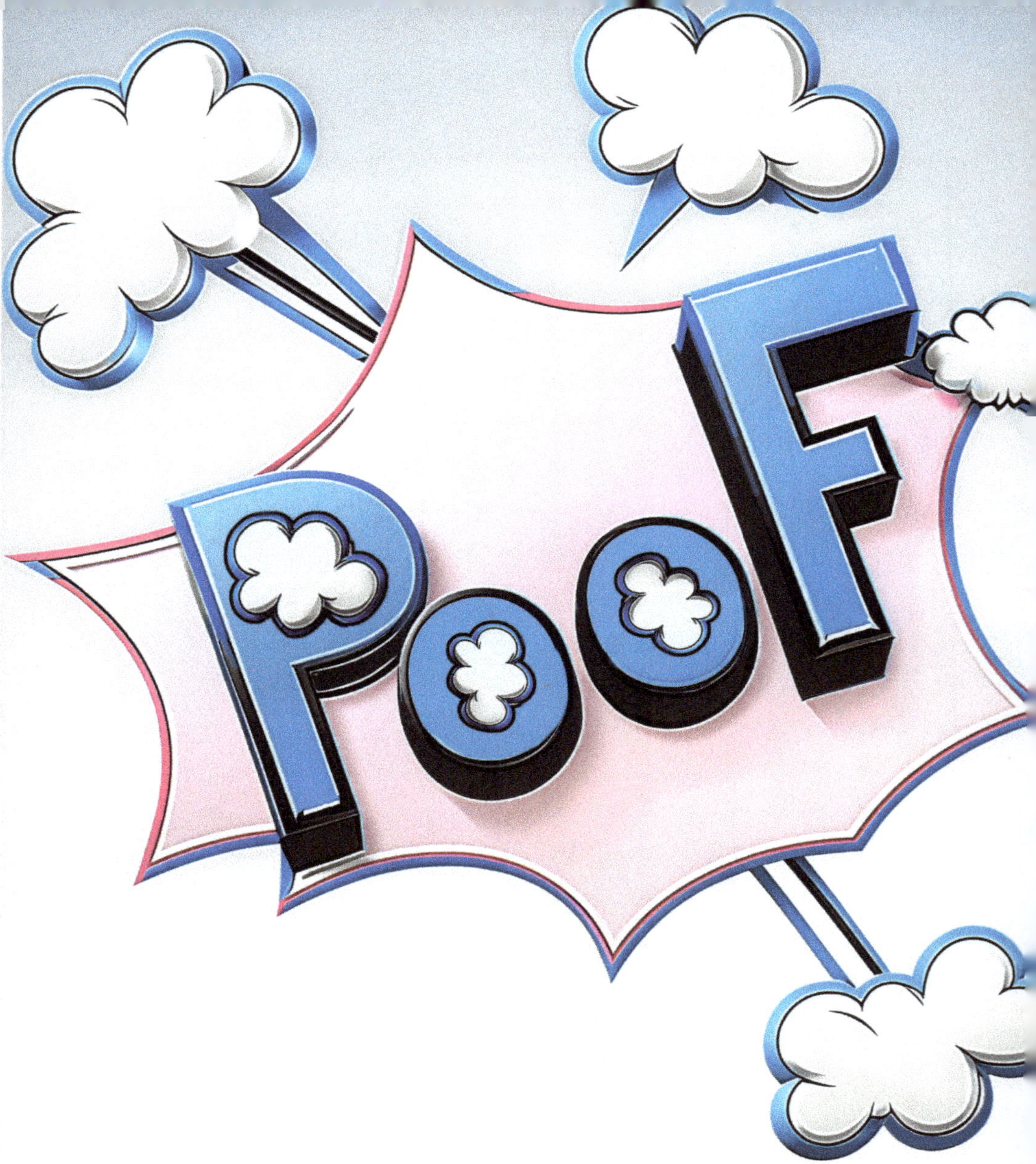
POOF

Tweet counted and counted until
she hit a pause.
"Where did the sheep go?" she
whimpered in a ball.

DEFINITION

Whimpered—a sound expressed by fear or pain

Tweet **rushed** to the window and called out to the Universe. "Universe, can you help me find my sheep?" Tweet **manifested** out loud.

DEFINITION

Rushed–hurrying; moving at a greater speed

Manifest–to make certain by showing or displaying

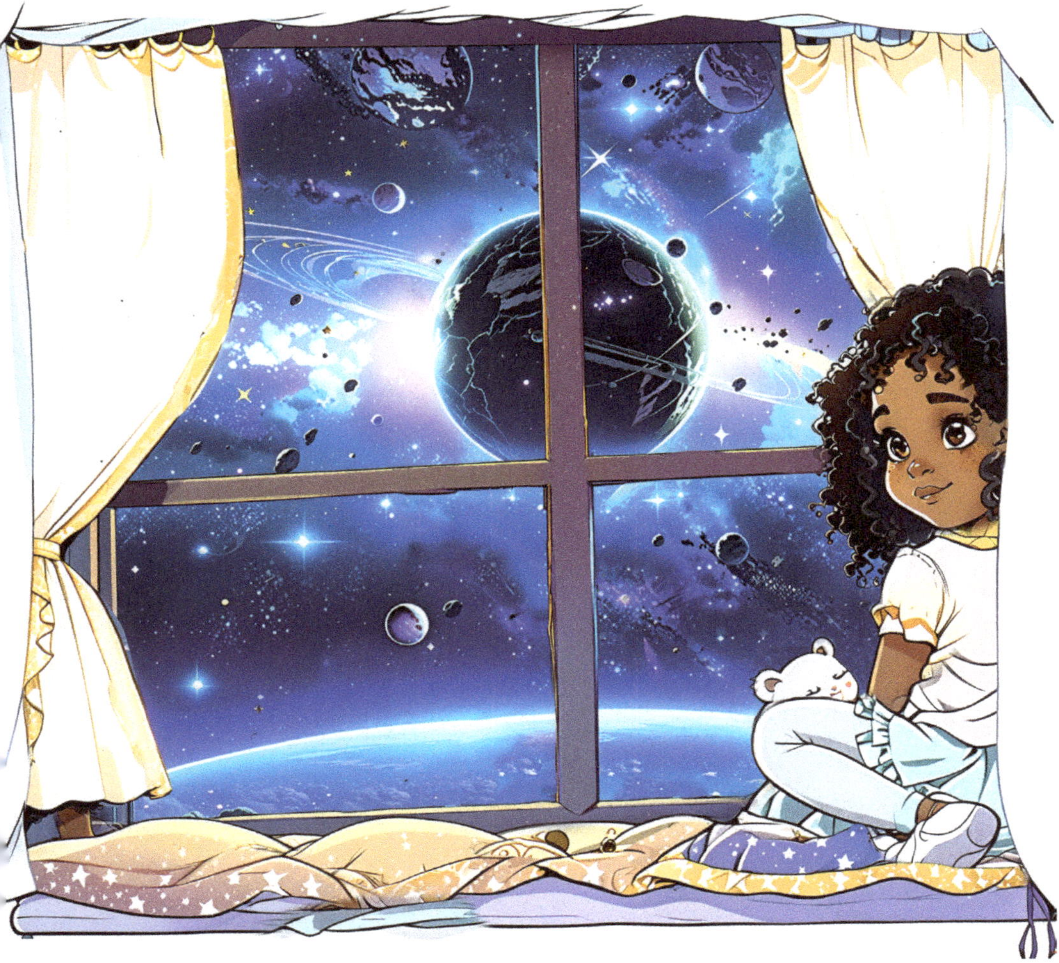

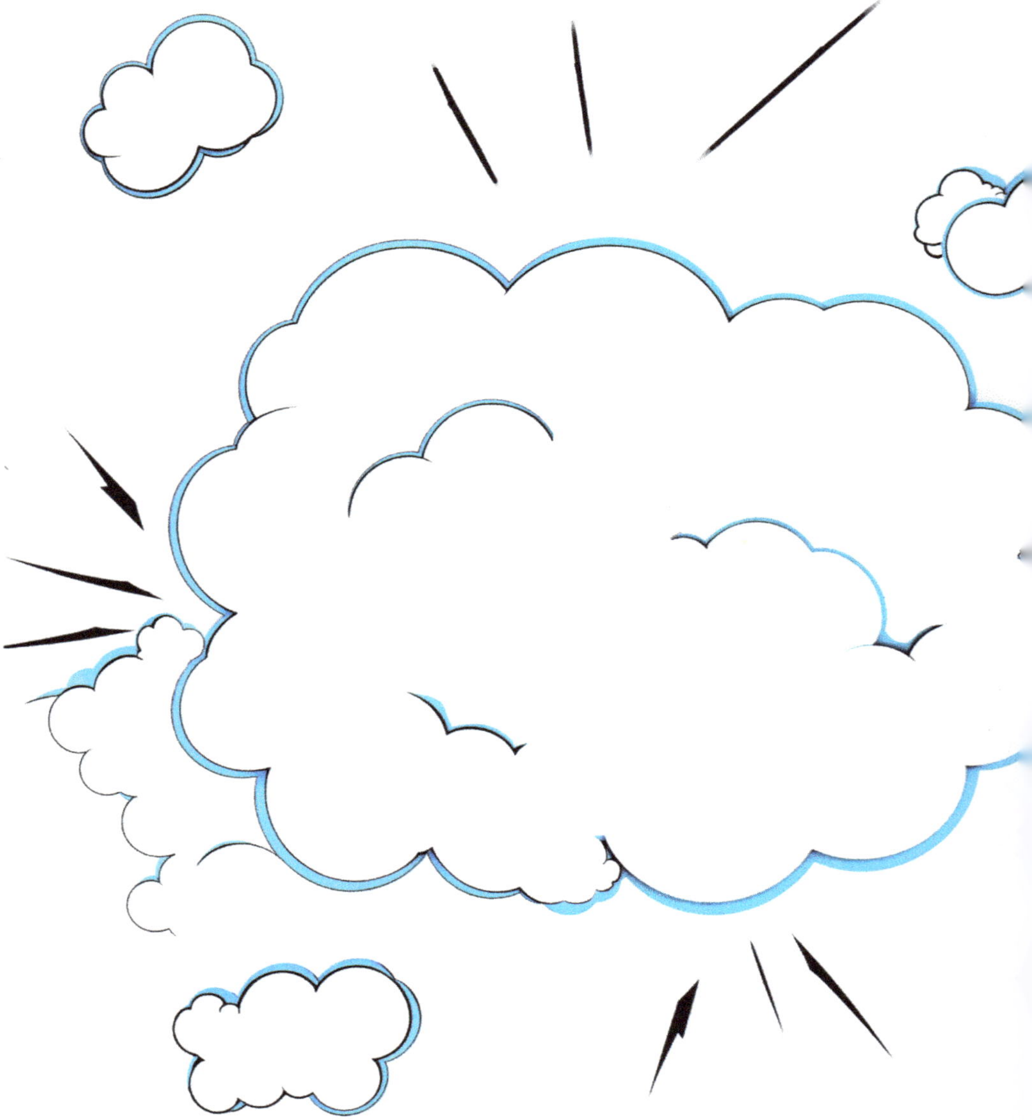

Tweet continued to speak in an **outraged** manner,
"The sheep have **vanished** from my mind; can you help bring them back inside?"

DEFINITION
Vanished—disappeared; ceased to exist
Outrage—strong reaction of anger, shock

The Universe said, "Tweet, I can help. We will travel to **Mars**, **Saturn**, and **Pluto** to help find your sheep and bring them home to you, kiddo."

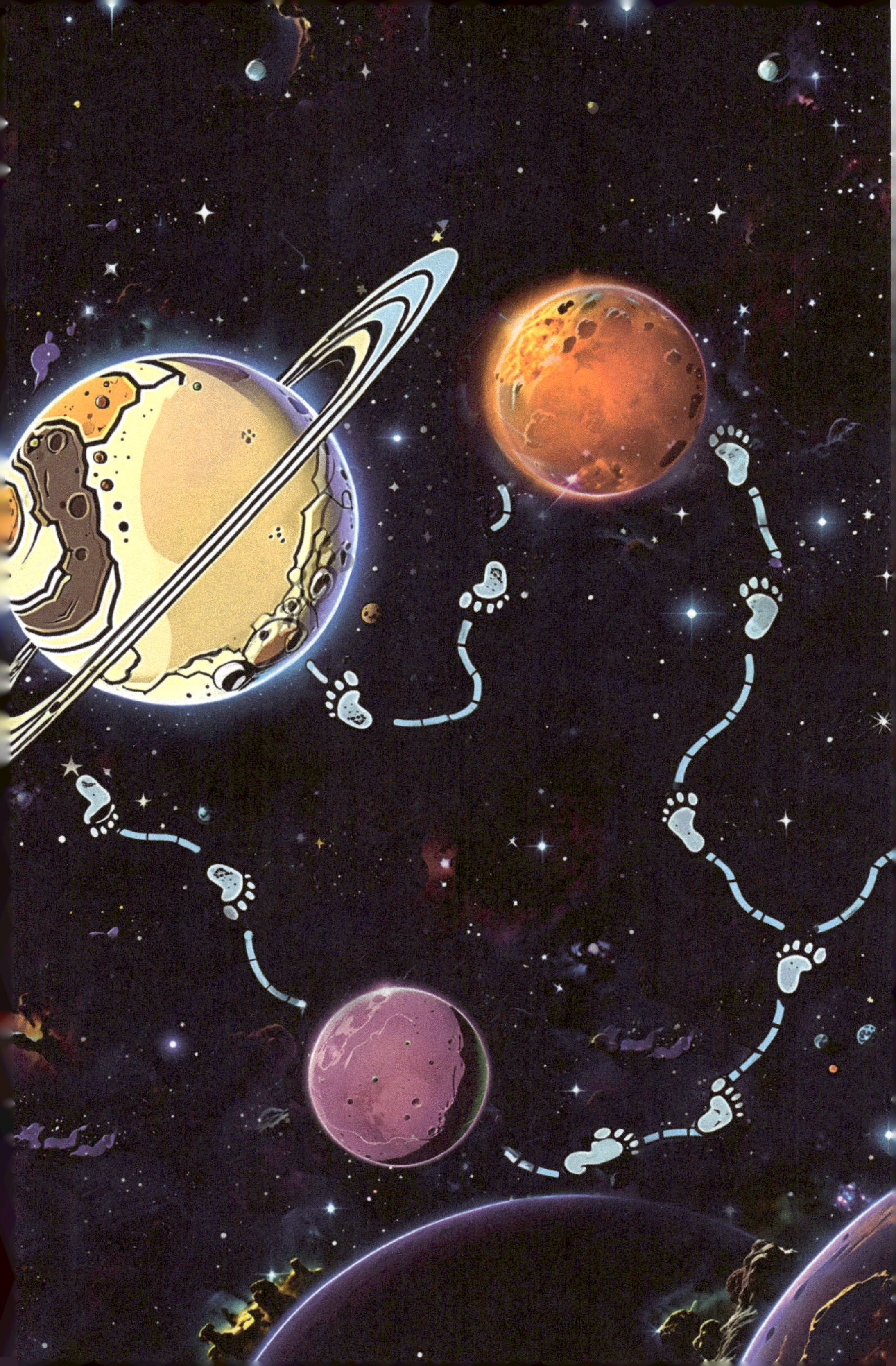

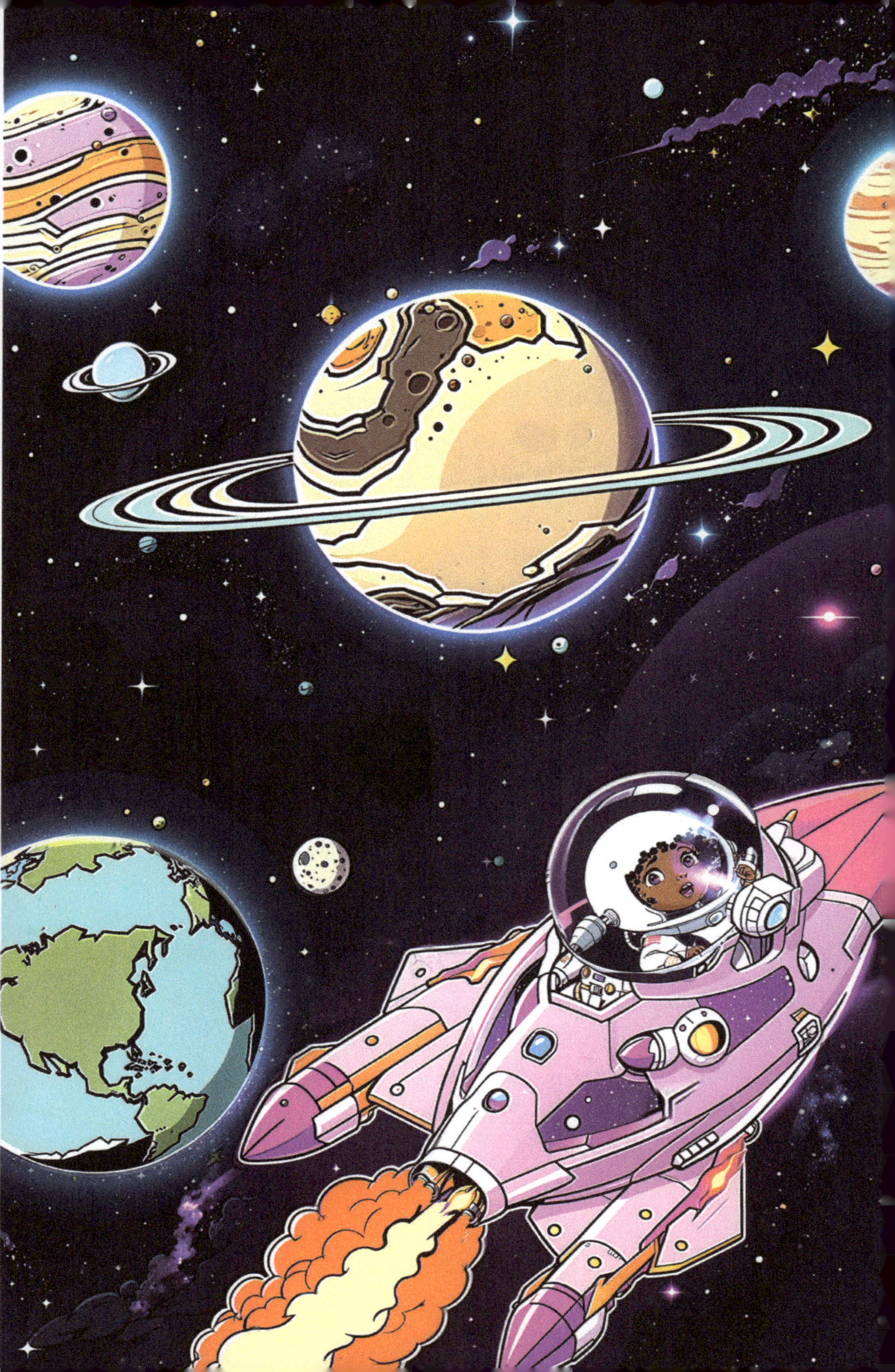

Passing the stars and the **galaxies** through space, There were no sheep around this **cosmic** place.

DEFINITION

Cosmic—relating to the universe or cosmos

Galaxies—billions of stars together with a gas of dust

Tweet was **overwhelmed** with the **Journey** so long, she gave up and decided to head home.

DEFINITION
Overwhelmed—defeated by a task or job
Journey—traveling from one place to another

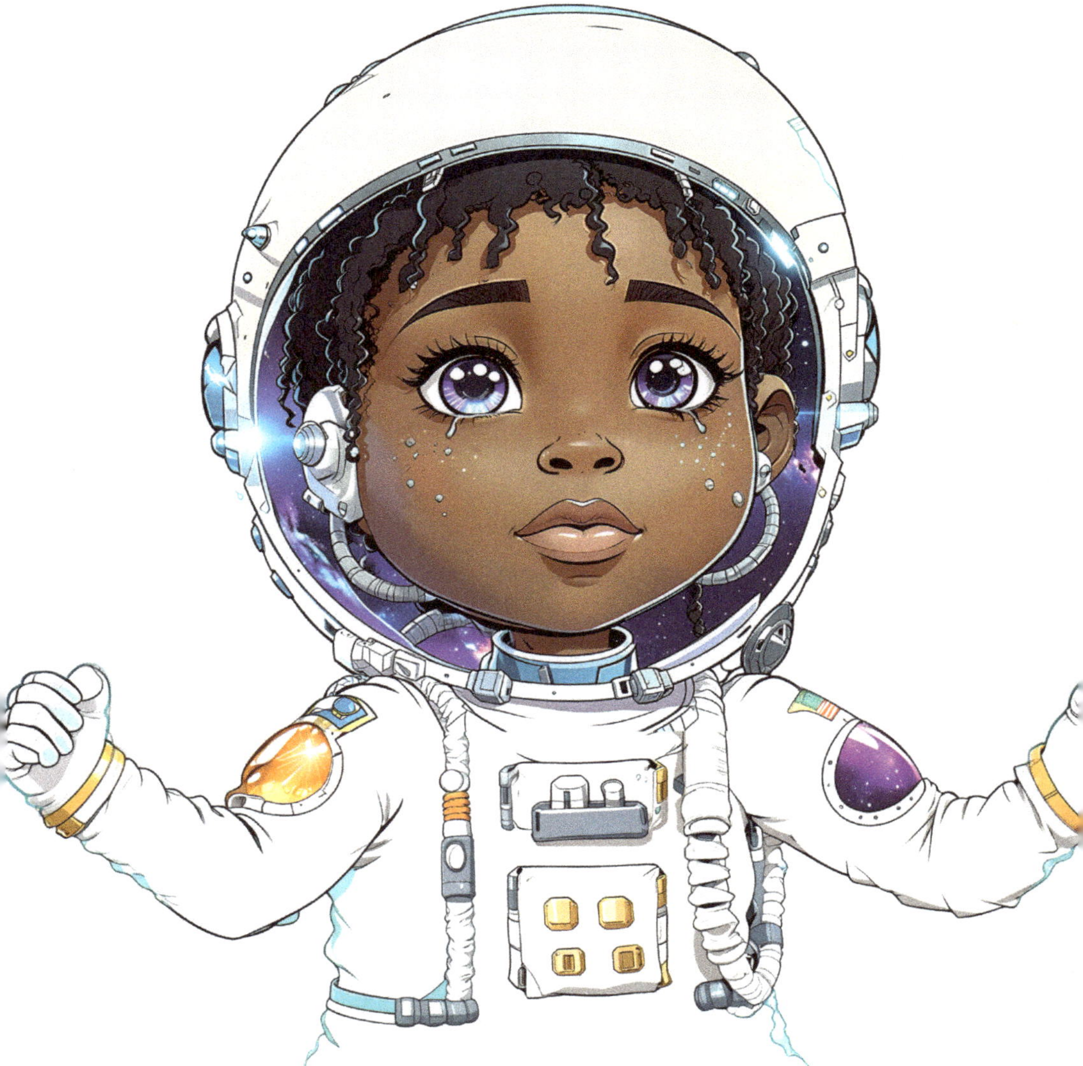

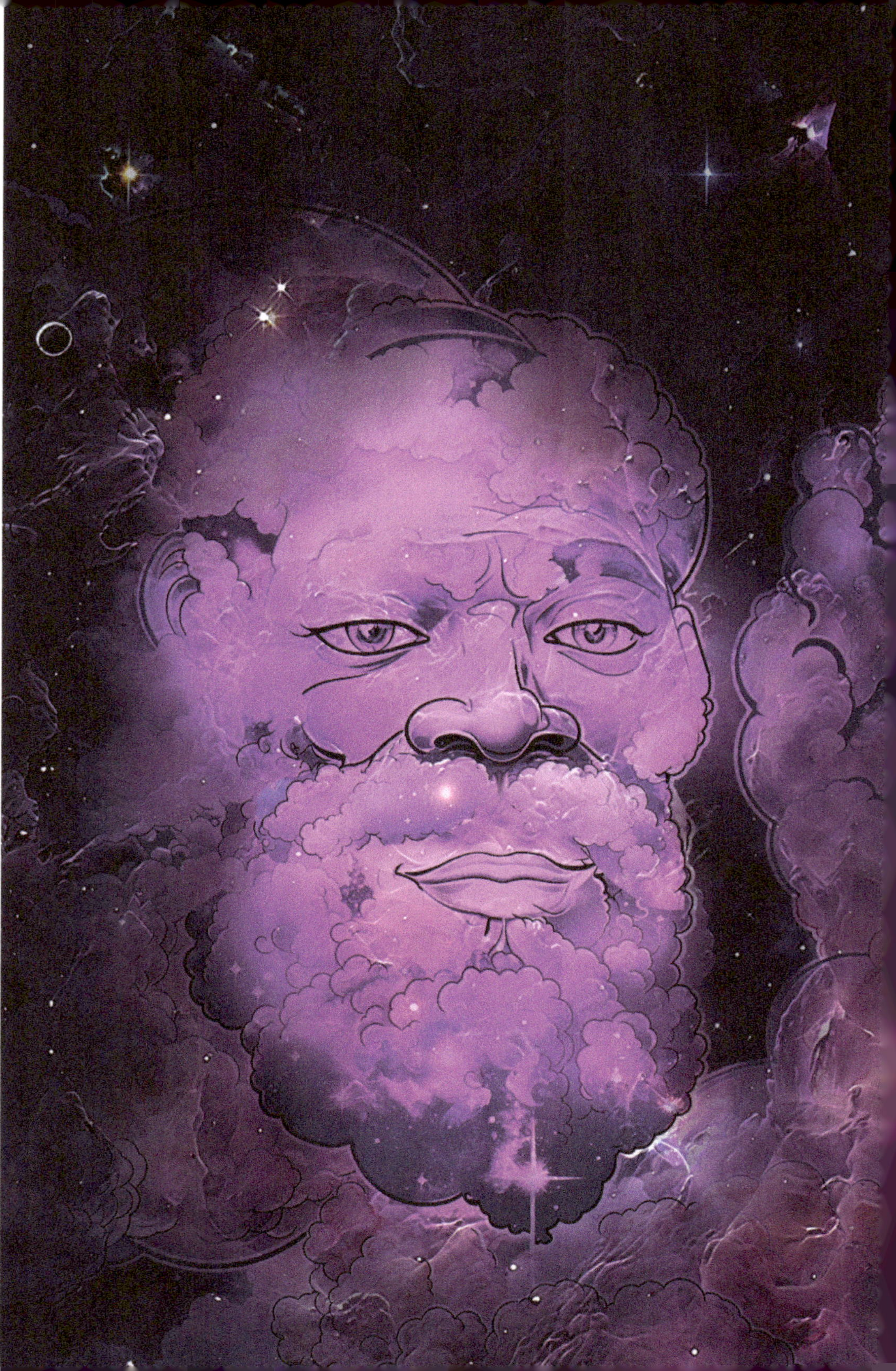

The Universe stopped her before she reached the door and said, "The imagination is within you to discover and explore. Don't give up on your journey. Keep **believing** MORE; **re-create** your **harmony** and **limitless** you will **soar**.

DEFINITION
Believe—accept as true
Re-create—create again
Harmony—agreement of ideas; consistent
Limitless—without end
Soar—fly or rise high above

"Tweet!" Universe shouted out. "When you go back to sleep, **remember** to **escape** your **thoughts**, and the sheep will **reappear**, **recovering** from lost."

DEFINITION
Escape—break free from
Reappear—come back into sight/vision
Recovering—return to a normal state of mind/ original
Thoughts—ideas/self-arising
Remember—recalling something that is necessary or experienced in the past

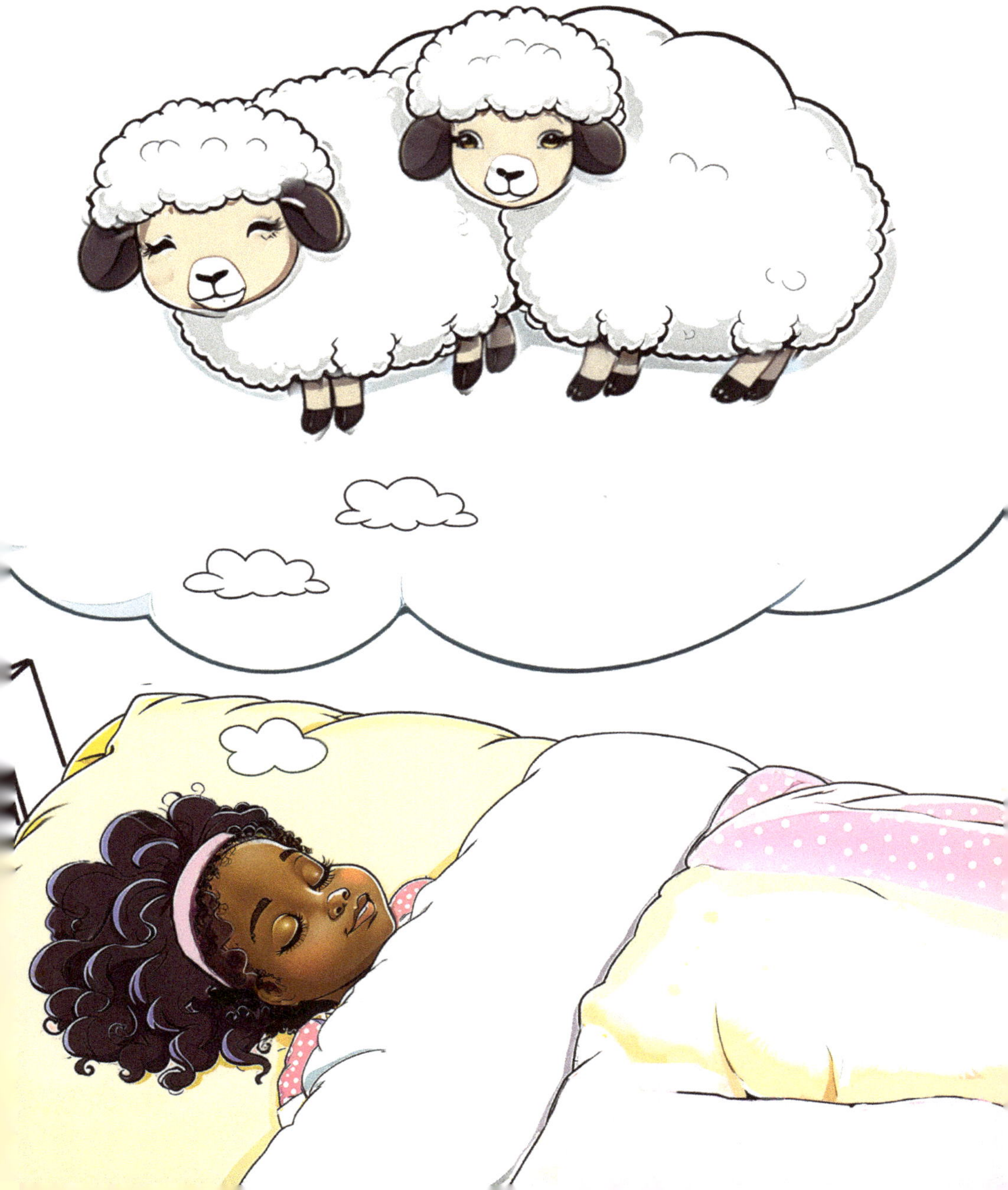

Tweet closed her eyes, escaping her thoughts. Tweet counted quietly and whispered this soft, "Come back, come back," believing in her words. The sheep then **manifested**, floating in the air. As the night went on, the Universe **peeked** in, and Tweet was fast asleep. The Universe spoke **boldly** into Tweet's window. "Be **aware** of your journey, own your truth, sleep tight, kiddo. Dreams do come true."

DEFINITION
Manifested—evidence of/ action
Boldly—confident
Peeked—looked quickly
Aware—having knowledge of a situation/fact

About the Author

Hello my name is LaTarshia, I am

an author and so much more...

My mom wanted her and I to

publish books together since I was

a young child.

Dreams can be created no matter where you are in life.

Manifest that dreams are possible and that believing is

power. Create your destiny and pioneer your adventures,

dear readers.

Printed in the USA
CPSIA information can be obtained
at www.ICGtesting.com
LVHW071705091124
796175LV00008B/106